UNDERSTANDING
EROI AND
HOW IT CAN HELP YOUR
ROI

UNDERSTANDING EROI AND HOW IT CAN HELP YOUR ROI

TERRI E. DUNBAR

CONTENTS

INTRODUCTION

It's no secret that investing in *employees* is a key factor in the overall success of any business. After all, if the Great Resignation of the post-Covid era taught us anything, it is that employees have growing demands and expectations from their employers, their personal and professional development being two of these. And yet, throughout my career as a Business School professor and the owner of a small IT consulting firm, I have continuously witnessed businesses' downfalls resulting from their lack of investment in human capital. This is what this book aims to address.

When it comes to *Return on Investment*, safe to say that most of you will know exactly what I am referring to – you invest in order to receive returns, and you subtract the cost of the investment from the returns to find **net returns**. The same concept can be applied to *Employee* Return on Investment, or *E*ROI. The goal of this book is both to provide insights into this process, namely to outline *why* your business should be investing more in human capital, and most importantly, *how* to do so successfully.

Indeed, investing in your employees is about more than providing free snacks, office parties and checking in with them one-on-one once in a while. Employees want to feel cared for, and part of this involves feeling like their career goals can be fulfilled by your organization. As you can imagine, this requires much more than a party with an open bar! With this in mind, this book will explore the various facets of EROI, ranging from how EROI differs from other metrics, to training and development programs, the role that compensation plays in EROI, how company culture and work-life balance influence it, and how engagement may be your lifesaver in terms of EROI.

Without further ado, let's begin.

1

UNDERSTANDING EROI

CHAPTER

UNDERSTANDING EROI

STARTING WITH A DEFINITION, EMPLOYEE RETURN ON INVESTMENT, OR EROI as mentioned earlier, is a **metric** that businesses use to measure the returns (financial) generated by the investments they make into their employees. This metric specifically includes the cost of such investments, such as the cost of training employees, their development, compensation, and engagement programs, and compares these costs to the returns (i.e., the financial benefits). The main goal of EROI is to showcase whether the current investments are bringing the returns expected. In other words, it helps your business determine whether the office parties are indeed keeping employees around, and whether they are contributing to employees' performance in terms of the revenue their work generates, or whether more efforts need to be made. The more information and data you have in regards to the financial returns generated by employee investments, the more you can change to maximize these returns.

But EROI isn't just about financial returns. Investing in employees can also have benefits beyond the bottom line! As a business owner, your goal should not only be to boost the bottom line, but should also consider the wellbeing of your employees as happy employees lead to happy customers *and* a more profitable business. The happier and more content your employees are, the more productive they are likely to be, and the less likely they are to leave your company, reducing your turnover and onboarding costs.

The costs mentioned above are rather self-explanatory, but the returns can be more complex. While financial returns can be measured in terms of the revenue made from employees, other metrics can also be considered, such as higher productivity and improved customer satisfaction. The greater your employee morale, the better your business outcomes are likely to be!

Unlike employee turnover rate and absenteeism rate, which can provide great insights into employee performance and engagement, EROI, on the other hand, provides specific information on the **financial returns** generated by employee investments. This is why EROI should also be measured, as while the other two metrics are valuable, EROI can provide metrics that are easier to evaluate in terms of wins and losses. At the end of the day, no matter how high employee engagement or performance is, the bottom line is still what keeps your business afloat!

To maximize EROI, your business needs to create a *culture* of employee investment, which means valuing employee development and engagement just as much as you value financial returns. As the leader, you play a great role in creating this culture! Let's explore how.

2

BUILDING A CULTURE OF EMPLOYEE INVESTMENT

CHAPTER

Two

BUILDING A CULTURE OF EMPLOYEE INVESTMENT

WHAT'S A CULTURE OF EMPLOYEE INVESTMENT? IN SHORT, IT IS ONE IN which your employees feel **valued, supported, and encouraged** to grow and develop both in their roles and in their career trajectory as a whole. Let's explore your role in this process and the strategies you, as a business leader, can adopt to achieve this goal.

Your role as a leader is crucial in this process. You are the person who sets the tone and who chooses where the resources for employee training, development, and engagement go. You are also the person who communicates the importance of this investment to the rest of the organization, meaning that if you do not choose to put it higher up on the priority list, no one has the power to do so. By outlining its importance, you are creating a *shared vision* for this culture – this shared vision is the first step in making your employees feel like their careers and role in your organization matter.

This culture can be created using many strategies, starting with the **prioritization of employee training and development**. Sometimes, companies will put the development of their employees on the backburner because other tasks and situations are taking priority. Now, of course, there are times where other situations are indeed more timely – when we arrive towards the end of the financial year, accounts must be done and sales must be completed. However, this brings us to another important component of this culture, which is namely that employee training and development should not be done on a "standalone" basis, but should rather be part of your overall vision. One conference or one workshop won't do the trick – it has to be at the core of your organization's priorities and this has to be seen on a daily basis throughout the various operations taking place in your organization. In turn, you will want to implement various opportunities for professional growth and development that aim to improve your employees' skills and productivity, but these should be part of a larger vision that puts this at the top of the priorities' list. Remember: employees are what makes your company run. Without their productivity and hard work, you are left with an empty nest.

A culture of employee investment is one in which employees feel **heard and valued** so they in turn feel invested in their roles. Think back to the first few jobs you had as a beginner in your field, or even the small side jobs you worked as a high school or college student. What made the difference between an "ok" job and one that you truly enjoyed doing? Chances are that the management style played a large role in this, more specifically, whether you felt like management saw you as a human being or as someone taking up a shift and who could easily be replaced. Making sure that your employees feel that they are heard is crucial. For this, create opportunities for them to provide feedback and input, whether this is through employee surveys or one-on-ones (regularly!), or group feedback meetings where the team can assemble and provide feedback. The goal is not to counterargue or to catch an employee talking badly about the company, but rather to value their feedback and see that their experience at the company directly impacts how dedicated they are to your organization's success. A healthy culture of EROI creates dedicated and loyal employees!

You also want to be **recognizing and rewarding your employees' achievements.** Marx once talked about alienation as being the result of becoming a simple pawn in a game where one's results and products no longer feel like one's own, namely because of the separation between the person producing a product and the person purchasing it from them. Put yourself in this equation, where you are the buyer of your employee's labor (the pawn, in this analogy). An employee does not want to feel replaceable, but they especially do not want to feel like the products of their labor goes unnoticed. They want to feel seen, appreciated, and heard, and this includes recognizing when they are performing particularly well and, importantly, **compensating** them properly. Likewise, work on setting up formal recognition programs for the "big wins" and make sure that they are accompanied by an appropriate reward. Then, incorporate the act of recognizing effort in your daily culture by publicly thanking employees, shouting out employees who perform particularly well, and giving credit where it is due.

With the arrival of Covid-19, companies have also seen a new trend on the rise: the arrival of the "work from home" scheme. Some business owners love it, some hate it, but the bottom line is – it's here to stay. After working from home for almost two years, and still doing so nowadays, remote work is no longer a special occasion or something that only digital nomads do, but it is an *expectation* from employees. While you may find that employees are likely to be less productive, research has shown that working from home leads employees to be 47% more productive, or even to work one more day a week than those working in the office[11]. After all, increased productivity is exactly what we're after!

EROI is improved through **flexible work arrangements**, meaning that offering these, such as the ability to work remotely or flexible hours, allows your employees to feel like they have more control over their lives, and hence, fosters a better work-life balance. The more control you give your employees to choose how they work, the more invested they are likely to be in their roles. Ultimately, employees who are dedicated to the success of their organizations will do what's needed to achieve this goal. And, as we've seen, this loyalty and dedication comes as a result of employees feeling like their feedback and enjoyment of the job matters. If you want your employees to be dedicated and to perform well, you have to invest in their happiness. For this, you need to give them what they want – and just like that, they're much more likely to *want* to be productive and to *want* your organization to succeed. Approaching remote work the opposite way only creates a vicious cycle in which your employees resent their work and, ultimately, your organization.

Finally, **foster a sense of community and collaboration** to improve your chances of EROI being positive. We spend a considerable amount of time at the workplace, so needless to say, the relationships we have must be somewhat enjoyable, and ideally *very* enjoyable. Invest time in building team cohesion, whether this includes team-building activities, social events, or collaborative projects.

Ultimately, a culture that supports EROI is one that especially provides employees with the ability to develop themselves and their skills. Let's head over to the next chapter where we will break this down into clearer strategies.

---

1   https://resources.owllabs.com/hubfs/SORW/SORW_2021/owl-labs_state-of-remote-work-2021_report-final.pdf?utm_campaign=State%20of%20Remote%20Work%20 2021&utm_medium=email&_hsmi=180908804&_hsenc=p2ANqtz-_QqLl-7bQetJbJYOdCoskUzS-r2pErrPvrTL353dUDu9e3aetTHyMlktMDf-N_opd0g0eg2lZzzzMM4MFaCkoOPa9Edt73hZO-7QXJGYUaOVMIId_nk&utm_content=180908804&utm_source=hs_automation

3

INVESTING IN EMPLOYEE TRAINING AND DEVELOPMENT

CHAPTER

Three

INVESTING IN EMPLOYEE TRAINING AND DEVELOPMENT

WHEN IT COMES TO TRAINING AND DEVELOPING YOUR EMPLOYEES, there are many strategies that you can adopt. This chapter will provide an overview of each of these. Ideally, your business should incorporate all of them into its culture, but this can also be done incrementally. EROI is not something that can be done overnight – it takes time, effort, and consistency!

The first step is to **identify your team's training needs**. Here, consider two aspects: what your employees want to learn and be trained in, and what *you* want them to learn and be trained in. As a business, your investment naturally should lead to returns that positively impact *your* business, but employees generally want to feel that they, as a person and professional, are growing. As such, do not limit your training options to what you feel might only benefit your business – an employee who feels that they are being invested in will be a happier and hence more productive employee overall, a benefit that trickles down to your bottom line. So, consider what skills your employees currently have, which areas might benefit from additional training, and where their skills can be developed further. You can run surveys, evaluate their performance, or ask for managers' feedback. Likewise, you can directly ask your employees: what skills would you like to gain?

Once you have established the training needs your training program will address, you can start working on a **training plan**. This should outline the objectives, methods, and resources needed. This is usually something that companies outsource to training and development companies as these can provide more information on the various types of training offered, such as e-Learning, group learning, and the like.

Speaking of which, offering a **variety of training methods** will ensure that all your employees, who may have different time constraints or differing learning styles, can each be accounted for. While Sandra may be an excellent learner in group settings, Alex, who has ADHD, may be a better learner online where he can choose to go at his own pace, take breaks when needed, and can go back to the modules that he may not have fully been able to focus on as he was distracted. Employees know what works best for them, so offering varying methods allows them to choose by themselves and to find a program that fits their needs best. Again, this goes back to the idea of being valued and one's opinions and needs being taken seriously – showing that you are flexible and can fulfill your employees' specific needs shows that you are dedicated to creating a genuine culture of EROI.

Once the training is done, your company should also **measure** how effective the training was. This is done by tracking employee performance metrics, including their productivity, the quality of their work, and so on, before and after the training. This may take time as the training itself may teach the skills, but the *implementation* of such skills may take a few weeks to be applied and noticed.

That being said, as mentioned earlier, **employee development and training should be *continuous*** as opposed to being one-time-only opportunities. As a leader, focus on encouraging your employees to continue learning and developing their skills throughout their careers. Provide training programs as needed and as wished for, and support your employees when they share that they are interested in taking on more responsibilities or learning other skills in various departments. Offer access to resources like books, articles, and online courses, and place an emphasis on how your organization values their enthusiasm for learning.

Alongside training and development, boosting EROI is also enhanced by proper compensation. Let's have a closer look at what this entails.

4

COMPENSATING EMPLOYEES FOR MAXIMUM EROI

CHAPTER
Four

COMPENSATING EMPLOYEES FOR MAXIMUM EROI

It's no secret that while training and development will show your employees that you care about their professional growth, compensation is nonetheless required for them to truly feel like their contributions are valued. No matter the number of office parties you throw, or the "employee of the month awards" you provide, if your employees feel that they work *too much* for *too little*, they will likely find themselves wondering whether they can find something better elsewhere – costing you a lot in terms of turnover and new hire training costs. On top of this, employees who feel that their contributions are not being properly compensated are also likely to lower their productivity to match their salary, as we have seen on popular social media trends.[2]

---

2 https://www.tiktok.com/@tanyaucoaching/video/7195283803173260590

We all know this: compensation is **crucial** to employee motivation and engagement. If you want to attract and retain top talent, you need to pay them what they are worth on the market. The right compensation leads to increased financial returns for your business because a well-paid employee is incentivized to continue performing to keep this wage, and because they are encouraged to perform well because they feel valued as paid employees. But compensation is not only about the final paycheck – it can involve other kinds of compensation!

Of course, you will want to offer **competitive salaries** so you can attract the right talent. It's simple economics – your employees or prospective hires will go elsewhere if they can find a better offer. However, you can also offer **performance-based incentives,** such as bonuses, stock options, and the like. **Benefit packages** are also highly valuable, whether this is a comprehensive health insurance plan, a retirement plan, or paid time off. And finally, employees value honesty, so be **transparent** about compensation. This helps build trust and makes sure that your employees don't feel that they're being tricked into being paid less than others.

5

EMPLOYEE RETENTION

CHAPTER
Five

EMPLOYEE RETENTION

WHILE THE BOOK MENTIONED THE IMPORTANCE OF RETAINING YOUR EMployees to lower turnover costs, there is more to this topic that we need to be acknowledging. More specifically, employee retention is crucial to the survival of your organization, namely because without it, not only are you constantly pumping out cash to have enough staff to keep operations going, but you are also constantly training new people, which is a tremendous loss of productivity. What if I told you that a high employee turnover can be overcome through proper EROI? What if, instead of focusing on hiring talents that do not stick around, you hired talent that you can train and improve through the EROI methods discussed so far in this book? Indeed, the more you invest in your employees, the more incentivized they are to stick around and stay loyal to your company.

But like any relationship, sometimes, you need to keep the "spark" up and need to invest a bit more effort to keep things going. If you, as an employer, stay stagnant and stop offering a quality experience to your employees, they are likely to also stop being interested in working for you. They will want to go elsewhere and experience something *fresh*, something new, just because it offers novelty. With this in mind, think about ways that you could retain your employees. How, you wonder? Think about what they *want* – not what you *think* they want. Chances are that your employees have told you exactly what they would like from you, either throughout your one-on-ones or in exit interviews. Employee retention is based on giving your employees a reason to stick around and to continue working for you, and this can only be achieved if they are incentivized to do so.

Consider what you *can* offer. For example, if the main complaint is that the wage is too low, you may need to find places in your budget to allocate more to each employee. You can also do this on a bonus basis depending on their achievements in the company. Otherwise, if employees have shared that they do not feel supported, that they feel overwhelmed and burned out, or something along those lines, then approach this issue as one of *culture*. You need to work on fostering a culture of support and collaboration where your employees' wellbeing is at the top of the priorities list, and, importantly, need to ensure that they **know this!**

6

MULTIGENERATIONAL WORKPLACE

CHAPTER

MULTIGENERATIONAL WORKPLACE

MULTIGENERATIONAL WORKPLACES IS A DIFFERENT ASPECT OF EMPLOYEE retention that tends to go under the radar. And yet, this is also a common reason why employees leave and go elsewhere. After all, there may be many jokes online about coworkers being "best friends" with their colleagues even if they are 50 years apart, but in reality, poor employee retention, when it is connected to multigenerational workplace conflict, can be very costly!

Your multigenerational workforce consists of employees from different age groups, each with their own unique perspectives, values, and experiences – as well as needs! The different generations currently present in the workplace include Traditionalists, Baby Boomers, Generation X, Millennials, and Generation Z, which when combined, can make it hard to figure out how to manage such diverse teams. Understanding and appreciating these generational differences is the key to promoting effective communication, collaboration, and innovation within the organization, and hence, it is the solution to many problems you may be facing in terms of retaining employees from different generations.

We have seen how the culture of your organization is the key when it comes to retaining your employees, but this also applies to multigenerational workplaces and does so in particular ways. First, it **enhances collaboration and innovation within the organization**. Specifically, encouraging your employees from different age groups to work together allows your teams to tap into a wealth of diverse perspectives and experiences. This gives space for the development of new ideas, creative problem-solving, and a more dynamic work environment that promotes continuous improvement and growth. That being said, for this to take place, your teams need to be ready to work with one another. For example, whereas older generations may be reluctant to take up new approaches due to fear of the unknown or because they do not understand the system, younger generations may choose to avoid speaking up or may dismiss older generations' perspectives on the basis that their views are outdated. Yet, this only leads to a loss of efficiency and the erosion of your culture – both sides must be willing to come and meet in the middle for cooperation to prevail!

Creating and nurturing a culture considerate of intergenerational discrepancies or misunderstandings is what makes the difference between a company with a low employee turnover and one that is constantly changing team members. Again, this results from the right investment in your employees. Multigenerational teams have different needs, and your way of investing in them must reflect this.

There are a few methods that you can adopt to approach this problem successfully. For example, you can **implement inclusive communication strategies**. It's no secret that some generations will be less able than others to understand fully how the most up-to-date technology works. This is nothing to be ashamed of, but it is something that needs to be addressed as it may lead to some miscommunication between team members who try to communicate and those who may not receive the messages altogether. To this end, work on having open and effective communication in your workplace so it remains inclusive. For example, **consider the preferred communication styles of different generations** and **use various channels** ranging from face to face conversations, emails, and instant messaging apps, so that *all* your employees are up to date and know what's happening in the company.

Respect and empathy should be at the core of your values as a company. It can be difficult for people living completely different lives and having even more different experiences with work to see eye to eye and to understand one another. So, focus on fostering respect and empathy within your company. For example, **address stereotypes and biases**, such as by **providing training and resources that challenge preconceived notions about generational differences**. You can also promote teamwork and collaboration by creating **opportunities for employees from diverse age groups to work together on projects**, to make sure that teams are not isolated by age group.

You may also want to consider **offering flexible work arrangements**. This way, you can recognize that your employees may have diverse work-life balance needs. Allow your employees to work from home or to work flexible hours, especially if they have dependents (e.g., kids that have to be picked up from school). This can also accommodate the preferences and life stages of employees that are from different generations across your teams, which makes them more content and keeps them around!

Going back to training, your aim should be to **design and implement training and development programs that cater to the unique learning preferences and career goals of different**

generations. You can even offer cross-generational mentorship programs that facilitate knowledge transfer and relationship-building among employees, since allowing different employees from different generations to connect, share knowledge, and share their life experiences with one another may be conducive to much more productive work than only offering training that is done separately.

As an employer, you are also tasked with retaining your employees, and this includes knowing **what kind of benefits they are interested in**. For example, you may want to offer comprehensive health insurance plans that cater to the varied health needs of your employees depending on their generation, as someone in their early 60s is likely to require different kinds of treatments from someone entering the workforce. You may also want to provide wellness programs, such as fitness memberships, stress management workshops, and mental health support, as these each cater to different groups of people. **Retirement plans and financial planning resources** are other ways that you can show your employees that you care about them even beyond their time at the company. For example, you can offer seminars and one-on-one consultations to help your employees navigate their financial futures and make informed decisions. Finally, consider offering some family-friendly benefits, such as flexible parental leave policies, child care assistance, and eldercare support, that can each help you retain your employees. The more you give them the experience and access to a life they can enjoy (i.e., through a wage and benefits), the less likely they are to leave and go elsewhere to find it, leaving you with a high turnover cost to deal with.

CONCLUSION

THE CORE MESSAGE OF THIS BOOK IS SIMPLE: IF YOU WANT HIGH RE-turns on your employee investment, your investment has to be worthy of such returns. Employees want to feel cared for, and they want to know that their contributions are valued. They want to retain control over their lives and hence want a work-life balance that is respected by their employers. They want to know that they are growing and becoming better employees as a result of working for your organization. Anything else puts your returns at risk, and it makes it more likely that your employees will simply leave and go elsewhere.

If you want real returns, you need to be ready to put in real work, and that takes real dedication!

On that note, best of luck with your journey!